THE
IMPOSSIBLE
MADE
POSSIBLE

THE IMPOSSIBLE MADE POSSIBLE

MAPPING YOUR DISABILITY LAW PRACTICE'S
PATH TO PROACTIVE SUCCESS

MARIA ELENA BERMUDEZ, ESQ.

CONTENTS

INTRODUCTION

The way that most disability law firm owners run their practice is a one-way ticket to burnout...

I know, because I've been there.

And if you've picked up this book, it's likely you have too. Maybe you've reached the point of no return, realizing that something, anything has to change, or maybe you're not there yet but can see that you're headed for disaster if you don't change course. Wherever you are in your journey as a disability law firm owner, I wrote this book to show you the light at the end of the tunnel.

The fact that you're a disability law firm owner tells me two things about you:

1) You're driven by a desire to help others
2) Because you launched your own business, you crave freedom and want to be in control of your destiny

Disability law is a unique niche. It's not a path to fame and fortune—if you were in it purely for the money, you would have chosen another area of law. This means that most attorneys who specialize in disability law are motivated by a desire to help the most vulnerable members of society. Maybe you witnessed the challenges a disabled family member faced or maybe you yourself are disabled. Whatever your story, your core motivation is to make the world a better place by advocating for those who may need it most.

But on a day-to-day basis, it's easy to lose sight of this noble mission and become crushed by the long hours, stressful pace, and draining lifestyle of this career path. You may start to question if you're actually having the positive impact on the world that you want to have. Your career doesn't fulfill you the way you thought it would, and you may feel hopeless.

What's worse, you feel that you're missing out on the freedom, independence, and flexibility that you thought owning your own firm would bring. When you read about other law firm owners working from the beach or vacationing abroad while their firm runs without them, you wonder, "What planet do they live on? How could that ever be possible?"

Running your law firm causes your health, relationships, and happiness to suffer... You've lost hope of living the dream lifestyle you envisioned when you launched your business, and you now just hope to get through the week as best as you can. If any of this is resonating, this book is for you.

When days are especially rough, or you're struggling to maintain a reserve, you may ask yourself: What went wrong? How did I end up here? Sometimes it literally feels impossible.

You're not to blame for reaching this point. In law school, there was no class on how to run a successful business, and even if there was, it was detached from the realities of owning a law firm. As a result, you launched your practice with little to no knowledge about how to run a thriving business without going insane. Meanwhile, the culture of lawyers surrounding you promotes the myth that those who work the hardest have the most success, encouraging behaviors and lifestyles that turn lawyers into workaholic shells of themselves—while the business itself may not even grow.

Without the proper education and mindset, a disability law firm owner may be doomed from the start.

But I've learned that even if you've hit rock bottom, it's still not too late to turn things around. As a disability law firm owner myself, I faced these same struggles until I came to a point where I needed to change my lifestyle, or else my health would seriously suffer. Through years of research and implementation, I discovered how to run my firm in a way that gave me the freedom and fulfillment I'd dreamed of when I began my career. Essentially, I got my life back...

I wrote this book to help other disability law firm owners make the same transformation. In the following chapters, I'll share a process to reinvent your law firm owner lifestyle, make your business more profitable, and open your world to options that you may have never believed could be possible. You'll finally be able to connect your business to your mission to help people, and you'll achieve freedom as a business owner.

But it's important to keep in mind - change is never comfortable. Some readers may be intimidated by this process and hold themselves back from approaching their business in a new way. To these readers, I ask: How much longer can you continue staying where you are?

Every disability law firm owner deserves a chance to have the business of their dreams, a healthy lifestyle, the freedom to create a self-managing firm and make a positive impact on the world.

If you're content with the status quo, feel free to put this book down. But if you're ready to end the suffering of your current unsustainable law firm owner lifestyle, read on.

CHAPTER 1

A Day in the Life of a Disability Law Firm Owner

It's Monday morning, and your alarm goes off.

"Already?" you think. You stayed up late last night catching up on work, with no time to relax and recover before the new week. You haven't even opened your eyes, but you already wish the day was over—you know the insanity that lies ahead. After mentally battling with yourself for a few moments, you bolt out of bed, get ready for work, and run out the door. You want to get to the office as soon as you can so you can begin to tackle the endless, overwhelming mountain of work that needs to get done today. As you sit in the morning traffic, you realize that you feel defeated before the day has even begun.

At 8:30am, you walk into the office. The red light on your voicemail is flashing like crazy… There's a stack of unopened mail on your desk… Your inbox is flooded with new emails… Down the hall, someone is arguing on the phone with a client who is already demanding to know the status of their case…Welcome back to the chaos!

Before you can even make it to the coffee pot, one of your team members rushes to your desk. "Can you get on the phone with this client? She has an urgent question and is yelling at me to get you on the phone…" You take the call with the client. Her question isn't actually that urgent, but she's clearly upset and you don't want to disappoint her and give your business a negative reputation.

After you hang up, you take a look at your calendar and try to organize your priorities for the day. You get interrupted a few times by calls from clients and questions from your team. Before you can even answer emails, it's time to get ready for court.

You call your client to prepare and have to play the therapist, soothing his anxiety so he's able to calmly testify. Then, you get on Microsoft Teams for the virtual hearing, in which you have to be on your game to cross-examine a medical or vocational expert. After the hearing, you get on the phone with your client again to explain the results of the hearing and what your next steps will be.

With the hearing complete, you sit down to write a brief that needs to get done today. Meanwhile, you're bombarded with calls, emails, and questions.

Around 2pm, you realize you're starving… You forgot to eat lunch because you haven't had a moment to spare. You scarf down a quick lunch at your desk while answering emails.

You get back to work, taking scheduled client calls, reviewing files, and managing your team, but before you know it, it's

6pm. You haven't made a meaningful dent in the work you needed to get done today, but you have an important networking dinner to run to. At the dinner, you do your best to schmooze with an important referral source even though you're exhausted.

Finally, you make it home and say a quick hello to your spouse and kids before sitting at your computer to attempt to finish the rest of your work for the day. A few hours later, you stop—not because you've finished your work, but because you have to stop to get some sleep before tomorrow.

Then, your alarm goes off, and you have to do it all again… and again…and again…

Is this really what you signed up for? When you went to law school and dreamed of starting your own firm, is this how you envisioned your life?

When you're a disability law firm owner, it's easy to feel like you're being beat up in every direction. Whether it's judges, team members, or clients, you feel like you can't make anyone happy. There aren't enough hours in a day to meet the demands of everyone around you.

Some law firm owners feel like they can't make their family happy, either. With such a demanding, chaotic work schedule, whether you intend to or not, it's easy for your family to end up on the back burner. You may not have time to sit down to regular family dinners, attend your kids' soccer games or dance recitals, or have a date night with your spouse. You feel frustrated because you can't be there for your family in the way that you want to be. You may be facing tension in your personal relationships due to the fact that you can't give your friends and family the time and attention they deserve. When people are facing enormous stress at work, it's easy to bring that stress home, and some law firm owners may be unintentionally carrying negativity, frustration, and anger from their careers into their personal lives.

But if anyone's needs get left behind in the chaos…it's yours. While you're trying to make everyone else happy, you don't have time to take care of your own health and well-being. You don't have time to eat three meals some days, let alone cook a healthy, nutritious meal. You may find that you're surviving on coffee… You aren't getting enough sleep or exercise, and living in a constant state of stress takes a toll on your mental and physical health. Most importantly…you aren't happy.

You may think all of this is an exaggeration but I lived it, until I applied what I'm about to share with you in this book and transformed my firm and my life… and I've spoken to far too many disability firm owners to know that this is the rule, not the exception.

Steve Jobs once said, "I have looked in the mirror every morning and asked myself: If today were the last day of my life, would I want to do what I am about to do today?" And whenever the answer has been "No" for too many days in a row, I know I need to change something."

If you're not happy in your day-to-day life, something needs to change.

The Grind

The way most lawyers do disability law is a grind. Most lawyers have 200 to 500 cases on their plate at any given time...When you add up the time you spend on legal work, networking, admin, and being in court, you likely work 12 to 15-hour days... These numbers are not sustainable...

The law profession also suffers from an urgency culture. Everything has to be done right now. There's no sense of priority, so every task is treated as an emergency that has to get taken care of right away. Lawyers face constant interruptions from team members and clients that make it impossible to focus on getting things done. The workday feels hectic, chaotic, and unorganized.

If you don't take action to change the way your practice operates, the law firm grind can become like quicksand... As the days, months, and years go on, the grind will exhaust you more and more until you finally reach a breaking point. I know because I've been there... And I've seen countless attorneys experience the same. But I believe you shouldn't have to hit rock bottom to figure out that something needs to change.

Albert Einstein said, "Insanity is doing the same thing over and over again and expecting new results." Yet so many attorneys hear their morning alarm go off, rush to work, and repeat the same endless slog that they faced yesterday. If you're not careful, you can spend years caught in this cycle. But the law firm owner grind doesn't have to be your fate... There is an escape plan.

CHAPTER 2

The Reality of Working with Disabled Clients

All day long, every day of the week, our law firm phones are ringing, and when we answer, our disabled client says, "I need to know the status of my case..."

You want to help your clients and get them answers, but they don't realize that getting information on a case from the Social Security Administration, one of the largest US federal agencies, is an uphill battle. It's not uncommon for an attorney or team member to spend 45 minutes waiting on the phone to get information from Social Security, only for the line to disconnect before they can even speak to a representative. Because the agency is so large and complex, it's easy for your case to get lost in the chaos. Trying to communicate with the Social Security Administration can feel like shouting into an abyss.

But your clients don't understand that, so they often become frustrated with you, not realizing that you're doing everything in your power to get updates on their case. Clients calling every day to ask "What's the status of my case?" can feel like an aggravating interruption, but really these clients are just looking for hope. When they perceive that you're not getting them the information they want, it's easy for them to become emotional and take out their feelings on you.

This means that, as if your workday wasn't overwhelming enough, you often have to face highly emotional confrontations with clients who are desperate, afraid, and anxious about their cases.

As a disability lawyer, your clients are some of the most vulnerable people on the planet. Many of them are dealing with mental health issues or a history of trauma. And no one calls a disability attorney when life is going great. You're meeting these clients at one of the most stressful periods in their lives when they're facing a serious problem they need your help to solve. If your clients face mental and emotional challenges to begin with, the stresses of their case are likely to exacerbate these issues.

Depending on their disability, some clients may have conditions that make it difficult for them to focus, which can be difficult when trying to guide them through the legal process. Many of these clients also have only a high school education or less, and symptoms which can further complicate communication with the firm, especially when it comes to providing the detailed information that we need to help them. All of these factors can cause tension in your working relationship, despite your best efforts, and can sometimes prompt hostility from the very clients you're trying to help.

Even if you intellectually understand why these vulnerable clients are reacting this way, it still can make you feel like your work is going unappreciated and that you can't make anyone happy. With all that you're sacrificing for your career, feeling like you can't even please the clients you're a mission to serve can be deeply discouraging.

Disabled clients are sometimes resistant to the legal process and can impede your work. For example, you may tell a client that they need to get treatment from a doctor so they have evidence of their condition, but the client might refuse. This could be for a range of reasons: they're afraid, they don't understand why this is necessary, they have a condition such as agoraphobia, or they're facing financial difficulties. Resistance from a client adds to the time it takes to complete any given task. It can be exhausting to go back and forth with your clients about simple tasks that attorneys in other niches might take for granted that a client would comply with, such as signing documents, answering basic questions, and providing medical records. You can see that the solution to the client's problem is within their grasp if only they followed your instructions, but due to a myriad of challenges they face, your disabled client may not understand that and resists out of fear, insecurity, or confusion.

Many clients fear testifying—their ALJ court appearance may be the first time they've had to publicly speak in front of an authority figure since they were in school. Most legal clients are nervous to testify in court, but when you're dealing with mentally disabled clients, it adds another layer of anxiety to the process. You may find yourself "playing therapist," easing your client's fears while simultaneously preparing to argue their case.

For most of these clients, everything is on the line. Most of these clients do not have financial safety nets in place, and they may be on the verge of foreclosure or eviction. If they aren't able to get these benefits, they don't know what will happen to them. You're meeting these clients when they're in survival mode, and they may project their desperation onto you. This is a uniquely high-pressure attorney-client relationship. They see you as the one who is responsible for determining their fate, and at times, they may lash out or even become argumentative during the life of their case.

The reality of being a disability lawyer is that, when you're overwhelmed, you may lose patience with your clients. When it happens, it can make you feel embarrassed and ashamed. These clients are some of the most vulnerable people on the planet. Many of them are rarely shown kindness from those in their lives. You likely went into this field to help these people, and you strive to be friendly and compassionate to them. Yet, when you're overworked, emotionally drained, and dealing with obstacles from every angle, one frustrating interaction with a client can push you over the edge and cause you to lose your patience.

Since many of your clients have mental health issues and histories of trauma, when you read medical records or other necessary files for a case, you're often reading about upsetting circumstances. When you have to take in this information on a daily basis, it can take a toll on you. It's crucial to take care of yourself and look out for your own well-being, but with your hectic life, you probably don't have time to take a step back and process your own emotions. If you're in an emotionally or mentally fragile state, it will be difficult to care for your clients. It's like the instructions given on planes: "Put on your own oxygen mask before helping others." To be the best advocate for your disabled clients, you need to be healthy, resilient, and at peace. If you're feeling burnt out or troubled by the disturbing information you encounter day-to-day, you won't have the mental capacity to support your clients, who are coming to you with their own emotional turmoil.

To eliminate the risk of losing your patience and to be the true advocate for the disabled that you wanted to be when you began your career, you need to change the way you operate your practice. The 12-hour days, constant interruptions, and lack of time to take care of yourself is a volatile mix that leaves you drained and on edge—in no condition to be the warm, supportive force you want to be in your client's lives. There has to be a better way.

CHAPTER 3

There Is A Better Way Forward

Sometimes, you have to hit rock bottom before you realize that there is a better way forward.

For many years, I lived the disability lawyer grind described in the previous two chapters. That lifestyle isn't sustainable, and sooner or later you reach a breaking point where you realize that something has to change if you're going to be able to last in this career any longer.

For me, that wake-up call came when I lost my temper with a long-time client who had cancer. Thankfully, we had established enough of a relationship that she forgave me, but I was so ashamed that I took out my frustration on this woman who was suffering through a terminal illness. "Are you okay?" she asked me "What's going on?" Clearly, it was evident to everyone around me, even my clients, that I was overwhelmed. I realized then that the stress that was consuming my life had caused me to lose sight of my mission to serve my clients. I no longer felt compassion for them, but instead saw them as a force working against me, adding to my infinite pile of work and constantly demanding something from me. Why was I annoyed by clients asking about the status of their case? Don't they have a right to have their questions answered? Don't they have a right to have someone fighting on their behalf? As soon as I recognized how stress had warped my mindset toward my clients, I decided it was time to make a major change.

I needed to shift from a reactive mindset to a proactive mindset. I needed to implement systems in my law firm that would allow me to calmly and strategically manage my workflow rather than constantly putting out fires and reacting to emergencies, always drowning in a never-ending deluge of work.

I also realized that you are the people you spend the most time with. Because I had to work nearly 24/7 to keep up with all of my cases, I was spending most of my time with clients. And as I covered in the previous chapter, disability law clients are in survival mode, often emotionally volatile, and filled with stress. I had placed myself in a vacuum, constantly surrounded by turbulent emotions. This left me unable to be a calming presence to my clients. Instead, I was in a feedback loop where I was taking on my clients' stress, only to project that stress back to them rather than easing it.

To solve this, I needed to implement more gatekeepers into my business so that I could take a step back from constant interaction with clients and be a proactive leader. I also decided to seek out others in the industry who were going where I wanted to go. I joined several groups for attorneys so I could learn how others dealt with the problems I was facing.

I realized that no one was going to make the changes I wanted to make for me, so I buckled down and invested my time in transforming my business. I cut out all distractions, reduced my caseload, and focused solely on my goal.

After auditing all the systems that existed, I realized there was nothing functional for this practice area. Out of necessity, I decided to create my own process that could be implemented for disability law. Though the lawyers I was surrounding myself with were a source of motivation and support, I realized that most of them, who worked in other areas of the law, did not face the challenges that disability lawyers face. They didn't have the phone ringing off the hook with people crying... I would have to take inspiration from their systems, but adapt them to meet the unique circumstances of disability law. For example, many of these lawyers were implementing software to make client communications easier. But in the world of disability law, many of our clients don't own a computer... I would have to create my own systems that were suited to the needs of the disability law demographic.

It took about a year to get relief. But after putting in the hard work to transform my practice, after years of stress and burnout...we were finally having fun!

My team members, even the newer ones, were empowered to take responsibility and make decisions. Like most law firm owners, I had grown accustomed to micro-managing my team out of a fear that something would go wrong. That risk-averse mindset is drilled into us in law school, so it can be scary to give up the reins to your team. But when I finally did, it was exciting for both my team and I... With the procedures I had implemented, my team was making less mistakes because I had outlined step-by-step directions with videos and links. Instead of coming to me every day with questions, my team could work independently, leveraging the resources I had built for them. It fostered confidence in my team members, and I watched them grow. These procedures finally freed up my time in a way I could never have imagined was possible. I remember the amazement I felt sitting at my computer, watching my new software and seeing my team members complete tasks without me stepping in. Finally, I could step back and devote myself to both leading my team and serving my clients, rather than trying to run my law firm like a one-woman-show.

Now, I can step away from my law firm without worrying that the phone will ring, a client will need me, or that there will be a fire to put out when I get back. Whether I'm attending a hearing, going into deep focus mode to finish a federal brief, or simply taking a break and going out to lunch, I can turn off my phone instead of constantly checking to make sure no one needs anything from me. I know that if something comes up, my team will handle it until I get back. I'm now capable of being a better lawyer, a better leader, and a more complete human being. Finally, I feel peace in my day-to-day life.

When you're stuck in the disability law firm grind, the life I'm describing sounds too good to be true. Years ago, when I was in the thick of it, I might have thought the same thing. But in the rest of this book, I'm going to show you how to reset your disability law firm so you can regain your life, empower your team, and make your clients happier.

This shift begins with a change in the way you think.

CHAPTER 4

Mindset

Several years ago, a friend said something that changed the way I thought about my life: "I finally realized that no one is coming to save me. No one is coming to make me work out unless I pay a trainer. No one is coming to make me eat healthier—I have to choose to. I can't wait for someone else to take charge in my life... It's all up to me."

At the time, I was deep in the struggle with my business, and her words resonated with what I was going through. I realized that no one was coming to save my law firm. I had spent years waiting and hoping for something to change without taking the needed action towards that change. Maybe I had subconsciously believed that someday someone else would swoop in and fix my business... But that's an impossible fantasy. If I wanted to save my business, I had to take action myself.

That's the first crucial mindset shift that a law firm owner needs to make before leaping into this transformation. No one else is coming to save you... This change will take hard work, determination, and sacrifice, but if you don't save your business, no one else will. When the going gets tough, remember that you're the only one who can save yourself, so you can't give up.

I also accepted the hard truth that I wasn't happy. I realized that I deserved to be happy... I deserved to run a business that I loved, that fulfilled my mission to help others, and that allowed me to live a healthy lifestyle. As the leader of my business, I am the only one capable of shaping its reality. If I wanted a business that made me happy instead of draining the life out of me, I was responsible for creating it.

Do you feel like you're waiting for someone to give you permission to change? Years ago, that's exactly how I felt. As lawyers, we've spent so much of our lives trying to please authority figures. When we're in law school, we try to impress our professors. When we're studying for the bar, we're trying to prove to an association that we're qualified to practice law. And when we finally begin our careers, we spend years trying to gain approval from senior lawyers so that we can climb through the ranks and achieve the success we want... But now, you've made it to the top. You're the owner of a law firm. There's no authority figure left to please but yourself.

You have permission to change... But if you're going to change, you have to change the way you think.

Overcoming the Fear of Failure

Most lawyers are afraid of failure. As smart, ambitious, high-performing professionals, we're used to achieving success. But when you're transforming your law firm, it's essential to let go of the fear of failure.

I've seen so many law firm owners remain stuck in the law firm grind out of fear. They worry that if they try to make a change, it'll backfire and lead to failure. To many lawyers, failure feels like a waste of time. But something I've learned throughout the process of transforming my business is that failure isn't a waste of time. Often, it's a necessary step to achieving success. You often have to try several solutions and watch them fail before you're able to realize how to achieve success. For example, I tried several client communication processes before discovering the one that worked for my business. If I had been too afraid of failure to implement these new processes without knowing what the outcome would be, I would never have learned which process led to success. Failure was not a waste of time, but a necessary step on the path to success.

I used to beat myself up for being "noncommittal." But what I had thought of as a weakness was actually a strength. The moment I realize something's not working for me, I get rid of it. If a new software isn't working for my business, I'll jump ship and try another software, even if I've only had the first one for a few days. I no longer consider that a waste of time and energy... If I try something and it doesn't work, I keep moving until I find the solution that works for me. It can take effort to defeat the classic "perfectionist lawyer" mindset and be okay with admitting that your first decision didn't work, but there's immense freedom that comes with letting go of the fear of failure.

The hardest part of change is making space for change. If you don't have the time, energy, money, or capacity for change, it's going to be difficult to make it happen. If you truly want to change the way you operate your firm, you're going to have to commit to making this change. That means that before you can start, you need to set aside the time and space in your life necessary to make a change.

Be a Leader

You're the leader of your law firm. If you don't take charge and make decisions now, the life you want to live will never happen. If you say, "I'll get to it in a year," you'll never get to it. It's now or never. You don't have any time to waste. If you've been trapped in the law firm grind for years, your physical and mental health are likely suffering. Your personal relationships may have taken a toll. Most importantly, you aren't happy. Life is only so long, and none of us know how much longer it will be. Can you really afford to waste another day, week, month, year, decade being miserable?

The problems we're trying to solve are not going anywhere. There will always be disabled people who need an attorney to advocate for them. These people need you. But before you can jump back in and help them, you need to step back and reinvent the way you run your business.

Are you showing up at work to be a leader, or are you just showing up to be a lawyer? When you own a law firm, being a lawyer isn't enough. You need to take charge and be a leader. Now, you may be letting your office manager or paralegal be the leader. But why should your business be led by someone subordinate to you? I challenge you to step up and be the leader that your team members and clients need you to be. Making this transition will take hard work. But in the following chapters, I'm going to show you a system designed to help you do less work in the long term.

CHAPTER 5

Assessing Where You Are

Before you can transform your law firm, you have to assess where you are today.

Are you proactive or reactive?

I believe the #1 source of pain in a disability practice is reactive communication. Rather than being proactive, most firms are always reacting to what clients need. They're always putting out fires and responding to emergencies. It makes sense why most law firms operate in this way. They never taught us how to run a business when we were in law school.

But when you have a proactive law firm, you're fireproofing everything so that you're in control before a fire can even break out.

Where are you on the Proactivity Index?

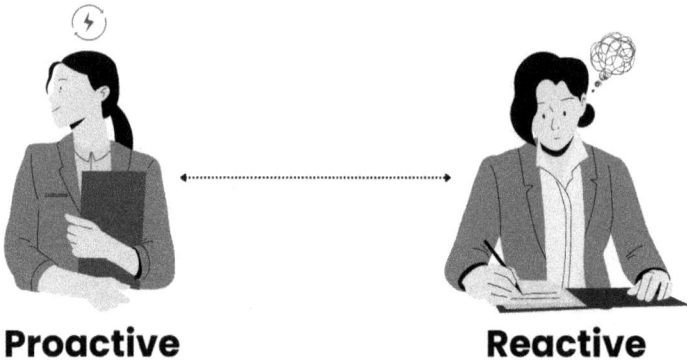

Proactive   **Reactive**

If you answer "yes" to two or more of these questions, you're running a reactive law firm:

- Do you sometimes lose your patience with team members or clients?
- Are clients constantly calling to ask for the status of their case?
- Do you struggle to feel well-prepared for court?
- Do you often arrive late to scheduled calls—or miss them entirely—because you're too busy?

If you answer "yes" to these questions, congratulations, you're running a proactive law firm:

- Do you communicate with clients when action has been taken on their behalf (such as when an application for benefits or appeal has been filed)?
- Do you provide clients with written or video information so they know what to expect ahead of time without you having to tell them?

- Are your files usually ready for court? Is all your evidence submitted a week before Administrative Law Judge hearings?
- Do you rarely have to worry about getting "emergency calls"?

To those of you running a reactive firm, answering yes to any of the proactive law firm questions may feel like it would take nothing short of a miracle. When I was running a reactive firm, I never thought it would be possible to run a firm without receiving emergency calls. Now that I've implemented proactive communication with clients, they no longer call to demand the status of their case because they already know it.

Assessing Your Current Tools

What software does your firm currently use? A disability law firm should have the tools for the following functions:

Information Gathering

It's essential to have software that collects and stores information from clients, specifically, a robust online form builder. For disabled clients, it's crucial to have a form builder that's disability accessible and language inclusive, with the capability to easily switch between languages with the click of a button.

Communication

One of the calls law offices constantly get is, "I got this letter in the mail from Social Security, and I don't know what it means for my case." To be able to help this client, they need the capability to text you a picture of the letter so you can look at it. But if you give clients your personal phone number and allow them to text you, you're opening Pandora's Box. You need software that allows clients to message you and your team pictures of documents via a mobile portal—it's especially beneficial if this software is connected to your case management tool. Then, whoever is online can answer the client's question at their convenience. Fielding a phone call takes ten to fifteen minutes, minimum, and it interrupts your day. By training your clients to message you, you can answer their questions more quickly and at a time that's convenient for you. You can also answer their questions better because you have time to collect information and get back to them, rather than trying to quickly pull together an answer while sitting on the phone with the client.

Case Management Software

Your case management software will store everything you need for your cases in one online portal. The software I use includes contacts, client communications, calendar, costs, notes, document generation and storage, time billing for fee petitions and interoffice communications.

Mail Software

This software enables you to snail mail clients with the click of a button. You upload documents into a system and on your command, a company will print and mail the documents for you. This is helpful for sending closing letters to clients and paying invoices. The service I use also issues and sends checks.

You can also use a service to intercept and scan your own mail. Your mail will go directly to the service, which will scan it and upload it to a portal for you to view and transfer to your case management system. The service I use also handles check deposits.

Faxes

Disability law tends to be fax-heavy because you have to deal with medical records. And government agencies. A digital fax software is much more efficient than physically sending faxes. The service I use allows us to send and receive faxes via email.

Record Retrieval Company

To save yourself time, I recommend outsourcing record retrieval to a company that specializes in it. I recognize that this may be controversial, and may not even be perceived as economically feasible for some. However, it lifts a major weight off our shoulders when we outsource a pain point to those with the time, resources and expertise to handle it.

Systems

Does your business have the following systems?

Intake

Despite the volume of prospective client calls that come into a law firm on any given day, we know that not all of these callers are going to be the right fit to take on as a client. You need an intake process to screen these prospective clients. Is the client's case something you can help with, or is it outside of the types of cases your firm takes on? Does the client have a viable claim? Does their claim have strength? Is there any risk if your firm gets involved with this case?

Client onboarding

Once you and a client have decided to work together, you need to complete the onboarding process. The client will sign forms such as a 1696, a fee agreement, and a HIPAA authorization form. In the client orientation, your support team will let the client know what to expect when working with you. The client will receive your client manual, get set up with your client portal, and learn the best way to communicate with you.

Client information retrieval

Through forms and questionnaires that have conditional logic built in, you'll collect the necessary information to process the client's claim. The client will also provide you with any documents, such as medical records, that you'll need to work on the case. Your support team will follow up with the client to fill in the gaps in the information you need for the case.

Claims processing

You'll file the initial application for Social Security disability benefits. If the application is denied, you'll file the necessary reconsideration and request for ALJ hearing appeals.

Hearing preparation

Your support team will assemble all of the medical records necessary to present your client's claims before an administrative law judge. You'll assess what happened in the lower levels of the claims process and determine how you need to proceed to strengthen the claim. You may decide to get medical source statements from specialists, and you'll prepare your client for testimony.

Hearing representation

These days, hearings are usually conducted virtually. You'll present the case to the administrative law judge.

Case closing

After the closing of the case, you'll "offboard" your client.

Do you have a detailed Standard Operating Procedure (SOP) for each of these systems that outlines the process for each step, as well as what language to use to communicate with clients about what to expect?

Your Team

The four main roles in a disability law practice are intake specialist, legal assistant, case manager, and lawyer. Each is responsible for running one or more of these systems. Which of these roles do you currently have on your team? Which systems does each person on your team operate?

In some firms, these roles are not clearly defined. There may be one person who's expected to do everything—or maybe everyone pitches in at random to get everything done, making the processes disorganized and inefficient. Without SOPs and clearly defined roles, your team is set up to fail.

CHAPTER 6

Setting Boundaries
(And Actually Keeping Them)

The Problem with this Area of Practice

In the disability law area of practice, it can be difficult to say "no." Your prospective clients are in desperate need of help, and attorneys may feel guilty saying no to cases or not answering client phone calls right away. Since you have the training and knowledge needed to help these clients, you feel a responsibility to do so. But after one too many instances of losing money or unintentionally taking on a case pro bono, you realize that saying "yes" to everything hurts your practice and drains your ability to help the clients you serve. Often, in trying to please everyone, you please no one.

Every time you fail to set a boundary, you're taking something away from someone you love. When you sacrifice yourself for your business, you hurt your relationships with others around you, whether it's your spouse, your kids, your parents, or your friends. To be a good spouse, parent, family member, or friend, you need to set up boundaries so your business doesn't consume your personal life.

My Early Struggle to Set Boundaries

As I made the transition from working at a large firm into being a leader of a team of my own, I ran into the same challenges that many lawyers face. There are simply too many demands for your time, than time available. Clients would pepper me with calls, emails, and questions all day and often after hours.

When you're constantly interrupted it's hard to get any real work done. The work you do get done takes two or three or four times as long because of the interruptions. My early assistants weren't much help. Despite having procedures that set boundaries, they lacked the confidence to uphold those boundaries.

They would allow clients to violate the boundaries I'd trained the team to uphold. Ultimately, I had to replace those team members with people who would respect and enforce my boundaries. It is good not just for me, but also for the team–they aren't forced to work in a reactive environment–and clients–they get my best, focused attention, instead of fractions of my time and attention.

Realizing that your business affects those closest to you is a big "aha" moment for many lawyers. Typically, lawyers have no problem sacrificing their own happiness and well-being for their careers. They may be resistant to putting boundaries in place, thinking, "I don't need to do that. If it takes 12 hour days to accomplish my goals, I'll push through..." As is usually the case, the positive qualities that drive people to become lawyers—ambition, work ethic, and discipline—can be our downfall. Most lawyers are willing to keep working and working with no concern for ourselves… But when we consider how this mindset around work impacts others in our lives, it's easier to realize that our "keep working until I drop" routine is destructive.

One of the first major boundaries to set is accepting that you don't have to take every case. Instead, you need to clearly define what your ideal cases and clients are and only accept cases that meet your guidelines. It can be difficult to say no when a disabled person comes to you with a problem, but you need to recognize that you don't run the only disability law firm in the world. If a client comes to you with a disability case that isn't the ideal type of case you want your firm to focus on, you can simply refer them to another firm or non-profit that does handle the type of case they have. This is actually more beneficial to the client. If you're stretched thin dealing with hundreds of cases, many of which are outside of your "target" type of case, you're going to end up too overwhelmed to be the best advocate for each client. Limiting the number of people you help allows you to help those you do take on as clients on a deeper, more complete level.

Take time to consider which types of cases are your target to take on and which types of cases make sense to turn down. For example, will your firm take on children as clients? These cases and the rules related to them require different systems, oftentimes making them more time consuming, but some attorneys feel compelled to take these cases because it fulfills their mission to help disabled children. Are these cases right for your practice, or would these clients be better served by a non-profit? Likewise, mental health only cases with insufficient treatment are difficult to win and may, etc. drain your resources. This is especially true if you are found chasing the client to maintain contact or they are the ones repeatedly calling you. Do you have the operating expenses to support these cases, or do you not have the infrastructure in place to take on these clients? I also encounter some firms who take on Spanish speaking clients, though no one on their team speaks Spanish, and they are forced to rely on Google translate to communicate. Though it's understandable to want to help, does your firm have the infrastructure to handle this added communication barrier, or would it be better for both you and the client to simply refer them to a Spanish-speaking attorney?

A client once told me a story: A woman walks along a beach, picks up a starfish, and helps it back into the ocean. A bystander says, "What does that matter? You just picked up one starfish." The woman says, "It might not matter to all the starfish, but it matters to this one."

Free yourself from the idea that you're responsible for saving every disabled person in the world. Each client that you help is like the starfish put back in the ocean. You may not have changed every life, but you've made an impact on many lives—and that's enough. As much as you'd like it to be possible, you don't have enough hours in your life to save everyone, so let go of that expectation.

Many attorneys give clients their personal phone numbers and let them call or text at any time. Communication with clients becomes an around-the-clock free-for-all, leaving the attorney with no "break" from work to clear their mind and rest. You may think that you're pleasing your clients by being accessible to them 24/7, but really, you're impeding your ability to serve them. When you receive client communications on your personal phone at random hours, these messages don't get uploaded into your case management system, so it becomes difficult to keep track of information and log next steps that need to be taken.

Being constantly open to communication means that your attention is always divided. When you're with your family or with another client, you're pausing every few minutes to check your phone and answer a message. And when you answer these messages, you're likely not always giving the best or most complete answers because you may be out and about—at your kid's basketball game, at dinner with your spouse, or at a meeting with another client—and unable to give your communication your full attention.

Most importantly, you're undermining your ability to rest and recover from work and have a life outside of your career. This hurts your family and friends because they lose your time and attention, and this hurts your clients because you'll feel too burned out to be on your game as a lawyer. By simply setting hours and expectations for communication—and keeping these messages limited to a platform that you won't check when you're on "personal" time, you protect your personal life and allow yourself to be truly present with those you love.

Leading the Way with Health Practices

In my consulting work with disability lawyers, one of the things I notice in many firms is that from the top down, the team engages in unhealthy practices. These become habits and can bleed into all areas of both the firm, its culture, and the personal lives of the team.

I get it...this is a stressful profession and you're working with one of the most difficult client populations in law. One of the most effective things you can do as a leader in your firm and in the profession is to adopt healthy habits yourself. Here are a few I believe are essential:

1. Eat well to increase your energy: Running on RedBull and getting "hangry" before your afternoon hearing isn't helping you, your client, or your staff.
2. Exercise to release stress and improve stamina: Sitting on Teams all day or in court isn't exactly the picture of an active life. Scheduling regular exercise during your week will release stress and send positive endorphins through your body. It will increase your capacity to handle the work.
3. Enforce your time boundaries: Clear time boundaries increase your productivity, give you the space to rejuvenate, and the time to work on the firm, not just in it.

Your team is watching what you do, more than hearing what you say. As you–the leader–adopt healthy habits, they'll follow.

What are you telling the world that your availability is? What office hours are listed on your website or on Google? Does your client manual state the hours that you're available? Some attorneys choose to operate on a Monday to Friday, 9-5 schedule and set those hours as the only times they'll be available to respond to clients. Other firms have a more flexible schedule and may want to simply tell clients to expect a response within 24-48 hours. You'll also want to set a communication sequence. For example, the client should message you through the client portal first, then, if their request is urgent and they haven't received a response in a certain number of hours, they're permitted to text a certain number to alert an employee to check the portal.

Will you accept phone calls? Some attorneys decide not to accept phone calls at all or use an answering service to schedule meetings. If you decide that it makes sense for your firm to accept phone calls, the firm owner and the attorneys should not be answering the phone—ever. Instead, implement a dedicated receptionist to act as a gatekeeper to you. An attorney can't answer the phone and also work on cases. Nothing would ever get done. I told one of my receptionists to think of herself as a knight wearing armor standing in front of me with a sword, there to protect my time. When a client calls and says, "Can I get Maria on the phone for a minute? I just have one quick question," it's my team's job to intercept and resolve the issue based on our standard operating procedures. You may also want to hire a receptionist service to answer the phone on when your core team is not available including nights, weekends and overflow calls.

You'll also want to implement boundaries around how clients are allowed to speak to you. In this area of practice, when emotions run high, it's not beyond possibility to pick up the phone and hear a client yelling and cursing about something. In my practice, I set expectations upfront that this behavior will not be tolerated and will lead my team and I to withdraw representation.

To keep your client-attorney relationship professional, establish boundaries around how you'll speak to your clients. For example, many clients curse when frustrated, and in an effort to make the client feel comfortable, the attorney may pick up a habit of using casual expletives to the client when talking about frustrations with judges or Social Security. But these words diminish the professionalism of your relationship and invite the client to treat you informally.

It's crucial to set boundaries with your team. In many firms, when the owner doesn't clearly define expectations upfront, resentment towards the team can grow if they don't meet the owner's desired standards of performance. This problem can be prevented by clearly setting boundaries at the beginning of the working relationships, such as, "I expect you to arrive on time at 9am. I expect you to be available and working until 5pm. I expect you to be kind to our clients. I expect you to follow directions when I ask you do to something."

An important boundary to set with your team is that personal problems get left at the office door. Of course, if someone is having an important problem such as a major health crisis or a death of a loved one, the rest of your team should know about it to offer them support and accommodate any absences. But too often, employees bring mundane frustrations to work, distract others with their complaints, and project negativity into the work environment. Set the expectation that, barring a truly serious issue, your team's personal problems are theirs to deal with at home.

You also need to make it clear that you need your team to be reliable. If you ask for something to get done, it needs to get done correctly and on time. Help your team understand that each of them is an essential part of a whole—if someone isn't reliable and leaves tasks unfinished, it will affect everyone else on the team. Just as your team expects their paychecks to show up in their bank accounts on a certain date, you expect your team to fulfill the expectations of the role you hired them for. As a law firm owner, you're too busy to worry whether something has gotten done, so if someone proves to be continually unreliable, you may need to replace them.

In the disability law niche, it's common to have referral relationships with other attorneys. These relationships need boundaries as well. Sometimes, an attorney will get into the habit of referring cases to you and making promises to the clients on your behalf, such as implying that you'll give the client special treatment. Other attorneys may call you at odd hours, asking you to quickly get on the phone with a prospect they want to refer to you. Setting clear guidelines about what kinds of clients you'd like to be referred, what hours you're open to communication, and that other attorneys can't make assurances to clients on your behalf ensures that referral relationships remain mutually beneficial.

The most important person to set boundaries with is yourself. As attorneys, we are used to pushing ourselves. But that stubborn desire to "tough it out" may actually be sabotaging your firm. Set clear boundaries for the hours you're going to work, and make sure you schedule time to get enough sleep, eat healthy meals, exercise, and relax with your loved ones. Setting clear time boundaries for yourself can prevent the guilt that ambitious, driven people can feel about not constantly working. Set time boundaries that protect your schedule and ensure that you're able to perform your best. For example, you may want to block off the hour before all of your hearings so that you have time to focus and prepare rather than trying to take calls or answer emails ten minutes before turning on Teams for the hearing.

Another way to protect your time is delegation. What are your strengths? What tasks in your business need your expertise and skill? Little by little, delegate any tasks that don't fall into that category to someone else. You went to law school and honed your skills for years so that you could practice law. That's a valuable skill that not many people have. Why would you waste your time answering the phone, scheduling appointments, or collecting documents? Gatekeep your time and devote it to the tasks that use your expertise. Everything else can be outsourced or delegated.

By setting all of these boundaries, your firm begins to be less chaotic, and you'll find that you have more time and clarity of mind. Finally, you're able to run your firm like a calm, in-control leader.

CHAPTER 7

Customizing and Integrating Your Tools

The Often Overlooked Importance of Your Toolset

Every master craftsman is particular about the tools they use. A woodworker can't use just any tool… They need a specific, quality tool that's tailored to their needs in order to make beautiful furniture out of wood.

In the same way, you need tools to practice your craft—running a law firm. Think of your law firm as your masterpiece. What tools will you use to create it? There is an unlimited variety of tools, resources, and software out there. With new tools being invented every day, keeping up with the latest technology available can feel like a project all by itself. But every lawyer thinks differently, so it's not about finding the best tool, it's about finding the best tool for you. What tools fit with the way you live, the way you want to run your firm, your values, your beliefs, your way of working, and your boundaries? What tools will allow you to do your job the best way you can? What tools will allow you to move in the direction you want to go?

Your phone system may not be the same as a prized chisel that a master woodworker uses, but it's integral to running your practice.

It's easy to say, "Oh, I'll just use the cheapest option," but the cheapest option is not usually the best option. Tools are an investment... They help you practice at a higher level and with greater skill because they remove friction from your work.

Without the right tools, the daily frustrations can add up... I remember that one of my main friction points was mail. It seemed like my firm had a never-ending pile of mail, and keeping track of these papers became chaotic. After going through a period of trial-and-error with several solutions, I finally found a mail service that worked for my needs—they received my mail, scanned it, and uploaded it to a digital portal that made it easy to keep track of. But if mail isn't a friction point for your firm, you may not need this tool... Implementing tools is less about taking a blanket approach and more about assessing what causes friction in your business and finding a solution that works for you.

Working with disabled clients is different from working with any other type of law client. You need to think about your tools differently. Many of your clients will not have computers, so all client communication needs to be "smart phone-friendly". The simpler your interfaces are, the better. Your tools need to be as friction-free as possible so that your clients, who may experience a wide range of disabilities and conditions, can easily use them.

To further eliminate friction, it's helpful to integrate tools with each other. These days many softwares have native integrations, and tools like Zapier or Make are designed to integrate applications so you can better automate your workflow. For example, if you integrate your phone software with your case management software, there will automatically be a record created of every phone call that comes in. Or if a calendar entry is created requiring the client's availability, a mobile app notification is automatically sent to them. Or, at the intake level, if a prospect completes an inquiry form online, a contact is automatically created in your case management software, along with notes, and a task list beginning with a task set for your intake specialist to follow-up. Integrating your tools empowers your team to complete tasks more efficiently.

The 10 Key Systems

Phone

What phone system do you use? Do you have an old school phone on your desk, or do you use a VoIP system.

Fax

What's your process for sending and receiving faxes? Are you still using a physical fax or do you have a reliable e-fax solution that provides sent confirmations?

Mail

What's your process for sending and receiving mail? If you are scanning in-house, are you using high efficiency scanners with routing?

Questionnaires

Systems for questionnaires are often overlooked, but they can greatly simplify your onboarding process. Social Security needs so much information from your client throughout their case: prior marriages, how much money they have in the bank, how many cars they have, what medications they take...

Keeping track of your client's answers to these questions can be complicated, and collecting more information from them if something comes up in their case can be difficult. You often can't rely on clients to supply you with necessary information as it comes up. For example, if your client has a medical evaluation and you have to object to something that happened during the evaluation, you can't rely on your client to realize the significance of this and bring it up to you. But implementing a post-consultative examination question-naire asking your client what happened in the examination is an easy way to circumnavigate this issue.

Disability cases often last two or three years, so it's also helpful to send case status questionnaires at key dates. This can help you keep track of changes in your client's basic information (for example, if they change their phone number or start seeing a new doctor). Without these questionnaires, someone on your team would have to call each of your clients to track down this information. When you have hundreds of cases, that can take a significant amount of time.

Texting

Texting is a great form of communication, especially at the intake level before you have introduced your client to the client mobile app. Most case management tools currently offer texting as part of their platform.

Case Management

Case management software alleviates the burden of day-to-day communication with clients. Every law firm owner dreads the phrase "Hey, I have a quick question..." A quick question is usually a 20-30 minute question, and they can swallow your day if you're not careful. But case management software allows your clients to see the updates you've made to their case status, and if they do have a question, someone on your team can answer it by typing three or four sentences rather than wasting time on a phone call. Most of the time, a client calling to ask about their case status is simply feeling anxious about the case. Having a place for them to communicate any updates when they want to can ease their anxiety and prevent them from calling you unnecessarily.

Mobile Client App/Portal

Most disabled clients don't usually have access to computers, so it's crucial to have a mobile-friendly client portal. Text only does not suffice as there are security issues along with limitations in sending attachments.

AI Medical Records Summaries

Manually going through medical records is extremely tedious and time-consuming... But recently, there have been tools created that use AI to summarize medical records. These tools allow you to review a summary in order to get the important facts needed to focus your hearing preparation or brief writing.

AI Brief Writing

There are also tools that use AI to automate advanced formatting such as creating a table of authorities and to pull facts from large records to support your brief writing.

A Virtual Office

These days, your office can be a URL... If you're working virtually, you can use video conferencing software to host meetings. The software will give you a URL that acts as your office, so when you want to meet with someone, you can send them the URL, they can click on it, and immediately you're on a call together. For disabled clients, clicking a URL is much simpler than trying to figure out a Zoom room code.

The purpose of implementing tools is to free you and your team from spending time on mundane tasks that could be streamlined by technology. With these tools in place, you can focus on the important work of winning your clients' cases.

CHAPTER 8

Building The Right Team

The 4 Roles a law firm needs are intake coordinator, legal assistant, case manager, and attorney. This doesn't mean that the perfect firm has 4 team members, one for each role... It just means that you need to know who on your team is covering each area. For example, you could have an intake coordinator, a case manager, and 3 attorneys. The attorneys share some of the case management responsibilities, and the case manager performs some legal assistant functions.

Take a moment to assess your organization and how the following roles are divided among your team:

1. Intake Specialist

Who is responsible for fielding the prospects? Who onboards clients?

2. Case Manager

Who is responsible for moving the case along the pipeline? Who makes sure that you have the information you need and that each step in a case gets completed?

Who keeps clients informed about the progress of the case?

3. Legal Assistant

Who manages the scheduling and calendar? Who manages standard operating procedure revisions and updates? Who manages the client needs that require additional hand-holding, like completing forms?

4. Attorney

The attorney reviews intakes, attends hearings, and drafts briefs.

Your organization is a reflection of you. It may be tough to accept, but if an organization is chaotic, it's likely that the leadership is chaotic. This doesn't mean you need to beat yourself up for any problems you perceive in your business, but thinking of your organization as a reflection of yourself can be a wake-up call that any change in your team needs to start at the top—you.

How to Get Started Building Your Team

Most law firm owners begin by doing everything themselves. At a certain point, they realize doing it all alone isn't sustainable, so they hire part-timers to fill in the gaps. Hiring part-timers can be an effective first step if you don't have much money to invest and need to get work off your plate—but it's important to be intentional about hiring rather than being in "survival mode." For example, some lawyers get overwhelmed by their workload and hire family members to assist them rather than taking the time to recruit staff. If a family member happens to be the right employee for your team, it could work out... But in many cases, lawyers select family members not because their availability, skills, and experience match the role, but because they're desperate for help and know that their family members might be willing to jump in and help dig them out of their deepening ditch. There are advantages to working with family, especially if you are still building. However, family relationships bring your personal baggage into the workplace, and it can often be difficult to establish professional boundaries with a relative. The challenges involved with holding a family member accountable without blurring the lines between your personal and professional worlds can significantly impede your law firm growth.

When you hire intentionally, you don't rush to bring someone (anyone!) on board. You take the time to reflect on what positions in your business you need to create and fill. You outline the requirements of that position and build processes that this new team member will be responsible for carrying out.

Alternatively, "survival mode" hiring looks like: "I'm so busy and overwhelmed, I need help quick...Maybe my sister can help me with client calls since she's home in the afternoons and I'll pay her by the hour."

How do you know when you need to hire and what position you need to hire for? Always look for the friction... If there's friction around some part of your business, take a look at your current process. Does your process need to be adjusted, or does this task call for additional help? Is there a team member you could assign this task to, or is everyone too busy already? You'll know you need to hire if there's no way to resolve the friction without expanding your team.

One big mistake I've seen many attorneys make is to use generic legal receptionist services to handle intake. With any other practice area, this decision could work, but a generic legal receptionist service will be completely unprepared to communicate with disabled clients. Since they have no experience with Social Security disability law, they don't know the right questions to ask prospective clients, even if they are provided a script. Prospective client interviewing in this area requires conditional logic, which is a skill and requires training and experience. If you hire an intake coordinator trained in your practice area, this team member will be able to get the information you need to decide whether this is a case you can help with or not.

Getting them Up to Speed Fast

With software and SOPs, it's easy to onboard a new team member. Once they get access to your tech tools and understand the processes outlined in your SOPs, they can begin to integrate into your workflow. But it's important to invest time upfront with a new team member. Taking extra time to train this team member in the first few weeks will prevent them needing to come to you with questions and clarifications later on. You need to help your new team member understand how you think, how you handle things, how you spend your time, how to best communicate with you, and what your expectations of them are. You can't expect them to read your mind after meeting you once in a job interview, so investing this time at the beginning of the working relationship is the best way to ensure your new hire can get up to speed quickly.

When training employees, I typically go through the processes that they'll be responsible for with them. I like to ask them for feedback on our processes—since they're the ones who will be carrying them out each day, they may come up with an easier and more efficient way to accomplish a task, especially if they have prior experience in the role at other law firms. But employees won't be able to make these kinds of recommendations if you don't spend time with them to explain the problem you hired them to solve and the tasks you expect them to accomplish.

SOPs are the biggest asset you have for training your team. I recommend keeping SOPs in an easily viewable online folder such as Google Docs that everyone on your team has access to. When you need to make a change to your SOP, you can easily edit the document and notify your team. Using software like Loom, you can create videos explaining new processes to your team. If the change is significant, you can schedule a training to go over the new SOP. It's usually not enough to write an SOP and send it off to your team. You usually need to sit down with them and let them "shadow" you as you follow the SOP, demonstrating how you want the task to be done. My team does this virtually, by screen sharing.

Making Managing Easy

When a team member is new, I meet with them once a week, but after the probationary period, once-a-month meetings with each team member tend to be sufficient. If we're working on a specific project or implementing a new system, these meetings become more frequent. For example, we are in the process of reviewing and updating some of our automated task lists based on the current rhythm of SSA's claim processing. This means weekly meetings at the same time where we discuss and workshop this topic only for one hour. It's a time commitment that will serve us well for the foreseeable future by reducing friction in the execution of our workflow. This can happen when follow-up tasks are generated too soon, or not soon enough.

The purpose of team meetings is to learn, grow and build the capacity of the team by instilling shared confidence in our established workflow. They are NOT bitch sessions... Don't let your team get into the habit of wasting time in meetings complaining about clients, Social Security, or their personal lives. Complaining doesn't get the team anywhere, but proactively identifying problems and positing possible solutions will.

Your team members should be meeting and training with each other outside of their meetings and training sessions with you. The purpose of meetings and training sessions is to empower your team to be independent so they don't have to interrupt your workday with questions. Train your team to rely on each other and their SOPs to accomplish their tasks.

Many professionals get so desperate for help that they're willing to hire virtually anyone who walks through the door. But it makes a difference when you hire someone who's excited about learning from you rather than someone who just wants a paycheck. In the interview process, spend time getting to know a prospective employee's career goals and values. Why do they want to work in the disability law niche? Though it may take more time and effort in the hiring process to find an employee who has a genuine enthusiasm for what you do, it's an investment worth making.

CHAPTER 9

SOPs to Empower Your Team (And Free You Up)

How many times a day do you have to answer a question from a team member about how to do something?

When you implement Standard Operating Procedures (SOPs), these questions rarely come up... Your team becomes empowered to solve problems independently because they have a thorough guide to completing all of their tasks. Your time is freed up, and you can focus on running the business without having to worry if your team is completing tasks correctly. And with SOPs, you never have to worry that a team member leaving will set you back for months.

Many people avoid creating SOPs out of perfectionism—they think each process has "a right way to do it." But there is no "right way" to do anything... An SOP is about documenting what you do now. Over time, you can alter the SOP to make the process better, but you can't do that without first putting in writing what your current process is. SOPs are a living document—they're not set in stone.

The Dead Simple Way to Create Your SOPs

The SOPs live in a folder in Google Docs. They're labeled as "how-tos": "How-to do a medical records request," "How-to process mail," and so on. Within the SOPs, there are example and reference documents along with videos and screen recordings demonstrating the step-by-step process.

There's a master table of contents document that helps team members find what they need.

I recommend documenting, at the very least, the following case stage processes in SOPs:

- Intake
- New Client Onboarding
- Initial Applications
- Reconsideration
- ALJ Hearing Process
- Appeals Council
- Federal Court (if applicable)
- Case Closing

You'll also want to document instructions, policies and procedures for handling client communications, mail, faxes, client resources, cybersecurity, internal communication, and other practice functions.

The Structure of an SOP

This is an example of the structure of an SOP. Some procedures will deviate from this structure for the simple reason that they may need more or less detail, given the complexity of the task, and the experience of your staff.

> Intro (What is this SOP about? Why is this process important? For example, an SOP for initial application might say: "Initial application is filing a claim for disability benefits on behalf of our client.")

- Procedure Flow (this is where you touch on milestones and responsible parties)
- Relevant questionnaires for the step in the process.
- Step-by-Step Outline of Process (with demonstration videos and example documents linked)
- What the Client Should Expect
- What's the next step, based on the outcome (linked to the next procedure): If the decision is favorable, let's move to this SOP. If the decision is unfavorable, let's move to this SOP.
- Corresponding Task List (these are the automated action steps generated in your case management software that will help you carry out the steps in your SOP)

Creating Your SOPs

I've found it's easy to jot down steps of the process as you're doing it in a "messy" document. Then, you hand it off to a team member to organize and clarify the steps you wrote down so that someone else could follow it. Avoid the pursuit of perfection. The most important thing is getting your process recorded on paper, and it can be revised and refined later. My team finds it helpful to have videos of me explaining on my screen exactly what needs to be done and how - Loom has been a great resource for this.

In the disability law practice area, the tasks each law firm carries out are nearly the same, but each practice may want to complete these tasks in a slightly different way or using different tools. It's best to start from a base or create your own base and build on it over time in accordance with your unique and transforming practice.

Keeping your SOPs current – the easy way

When you start a new exercise routine, in order to see results, you have to be consistent. SOPs follow the same principle. They're not "one and done." You can't finish them in an afternoon and then use them for the rest of your career. Instead, you have to consistently review and update your SOPs to refine your processes.

Years ago, my first legal job was at a large corporate law firm. I remember our SOPs were written in an enormous book that felt like the Holy Grail.

But these days, SOPs don't have to be set in stone in a fancy book that sits on a pedestal in the office. They can be interactive, living documents. Everyone on your team has easy, free access to Google Docs, so it's easy to build digital SOPs that can be updated as needed—when the law changes, when your team changes, or when you discover a way to make your procedure more efficient. You can set editing and commenting permissions so that the correct team members can update the document or suggest changes. If your team reads the SOP and doesn't know how to completely carry out a task based on what's written, they can tag you so you can add further clarity to the document and prevent any issues or misunderstandings.

I recommend calendaring SOP revisions throughout the year. During these meetings, you and your team will review the SOPs and ensure they reflect the way you've been doing things.

SOP revisions work best when delegated to your team, though you're always there to review and approve changes.

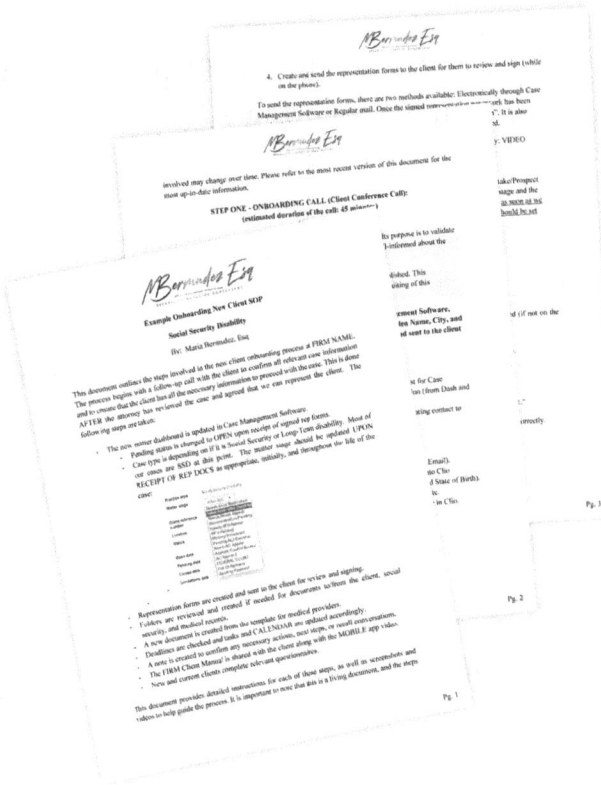

Example SOP - SSD Intake Investigation Guide

Essential Steps for New Prospective Client Management

The initial interaction with prospective clients is pivotal in the field of Social Security disability law. Establishing a thorough and professional intake process is crucial for any law firm in this area. The following provides a general guideline for managing new prospective clients effectively.

Step 1: Establishing the First Contact

The first contact with a prospective client is more than a mere exchange; it's the foundation of a potential long-term professional relationship (sometimes 2 years or more!). Here are the key steps:

- Client Record Creation: Immediately create a new contact record in a CRM or legal case management system upon receiving an inquiry. This is vital for tracking communication and ensuring consistent follow-up.
- Handling Consultation Requests: When a case evaluation request is received, promptly notify the responsible attorney and create a task in the case management system. This ensures that the request is efficiently managed.
- Intake Interview: If the case seems viable, conduct an Intake Interview to gather essential information. This step is fundamental for a thorough initial case evaluation.

Step 2: Detailed Information Gathering

A comprehensive gathering of information is necessary for evaluating the case accurately:

- Standard Communication Scripts: Utilize standardized scripts for responding to case evaluation requests. Clearly explain the case evaluation process to set transparent and realistic expectations.
- Intake Review Process: The attorney will use the information from the Intake Investigation to assess whether to proceed with the case. For positive evaluations, create a pending matter in the case management software. If the case is not pursued, maintain a record of the communication.

Step 3: Making the Case Acceptance Decision

Determining whether to take on a case involves critical consideration:

- Identifying a Disability Theory: Ensure each case adheres to a viable disability theory, such as Medical-Vocational Guidelines or Listing Level Impairment. This approach helps in selecting cases with a higher chance of success.
- Organizing Task Lists and Case Status: For accepted cases, systematically create task lists and update case statuses in the case management software for efficient management.
- Referral and Decline Procedures: If a case is not accepted, provide referrals to reliable legal services.

- Appeals: For appeals, collect all pertinent decision documentation for a thorough evaluation. Ensure that the evaluation takes place in accordance with any applicable appeal deadlines.

Conclusion: Excelling in Potential Case Evaluation for Disability Cases

This SOP is not just a set of procedures but a framework for ensuring excellence in client service. By diligently following these steps, a disability law firm can guarantee that each new prospective client is treated with professionalism and efficiency. The goal is to provide superior service that leads to successful case outcomes and positive client experiences.

Example Intake Task List:

1 - Please Contact New Prospect (Intake Specialist)
2 - Attorney Review of Prospective Case (Atty Task)
3 - Follow up with prospect (IS Task)
4 - Final Review of Intake - Accept or Decline Rep
5 - Onboarding or Close (IS Task)

Each of these tasks has an associated timeline, resources, questionnaire links and more specific instructions in the software task list.

CHAPTER 10

Training Your Clients

You not only have to train your team, you have to train your clients, too.

You want compliant clients. Clients who will trust in you and follow your systems and processes. You don't want your clients to inadvertently sabotage their cases by impeding your work.

Training your clients will cut your call volume. Most law firms handle all client education reactively, through one-on-one phone calls. Rather than creating a system to educate clients proactively through documents and videos, clients call day in and day out with questions. When you implement client guides, the call volume goes down. Your clients already have the information, so they don't need to ask you questions. Often, these documents provide more information than you would have been able to in a phone call. Before, they would have to call back again and again because your answers would prompt another question.

The disability benefits system is complicated...it shouldn't be, but it is. We're dealing with public benefits, but to this day, if you ask the average American who qualifies for disability benefits under the Social Security Act, most people wouldn't know. Some judges have a hard time articulating the definition of disability themselves. Although Social Security is a federal benefit program, it's very subjective, and its eligibility requirements are not clearly articulated. Often, it depends on how the state agency and judge look at a case. Many times, prospects come to attorneys because they want to be educated on who qualifies for benefits. Creating processes to educate your clients will ease their confusion and help you help them.

Establish expectations for the process upfront.

- How should clients communicate with you?
- Which communication platforms will you use?
- What hours are okay for the client to contact you?

Let the client know that at the beginning of the process, they'll likely hear from your team a lot as you collect information to begin working on their case. But after that initial stage, there may be long periods where you don't need to communicate with the client because you're waiting for Social Security to process the application. If you let the clients know about this upfront, they won't worry when they don't hear from you for several weeks and will understand that you're going to update them as soon as you get a response from Social Security.

Many clients don't know the full picture of what an attorney does. If you educate your clients upfront about your role, it keeps their expectations in line with reality and prevents conflict later on.

You'll also want to provide answers upfront for "frequently asked questions" such as "Can I claim unemployment while my claim is pending? Can I work while my claim is pending?" When your firm was reactive, you may have had to answer the same question from ten different clients in a week, but providing easily accessible information on these topics eliminates the need for a phone call.

It's easy to deliver client resource guides as documents and videos. For example, most clients are sent to a consultative examination by the Social Security Administration. To prepare clients for this examination, we'll send clients a document that explains why Social Security is asking them to go to the examination and outlines what to expect. The document will link to the Social Security Administration's website for more information, and it may include a link to a brief video of a team member answering common questions.

Nine times out of ten, client resource guides eliminate the need for one-on-one phone calls, but it's a good idea to let clients know that if they have further questions after reviewing your materials, a team member would be happy to get on the phone with them.

Can I work while going through the disability claim process?

The simple answer is yes. You can work and make up to $1,550 gross income (before taxes), which is known as SGA (Substantial Gainful Activity). That amount is set for 2024 and changes yearly. This amount is different in cases of severe vision impairment.

While the Social Security Rules allow you to work while claiming disability benefits, the rules are very detailed and it can definitely complicate the process. If you plan to work, or have returned to work, we should arrange a call to discuss the hours you're working, the nature of the work, the circumstances, and if you're getting any accommodations, etc. All of those factors should be explored for your specific case.

Please note, if you are making over SGA, Social Security will likely deny your claim without considering your physical and mental conditions.

You can learn more about this by watching this video:

Other resources:
1. Our blog post.
2. SSA.

CHAPTER 11

Keeping Your Practice Operating System Up to Date

To keep your practice operating system up to date, you need to empower your team to drive the updates. Create a workplace culture where your team isn't afraid to speak up when they notice that something on a Standard Operating Procedure (SOP) needs to be changed. Ensure that your team knows that SOPs are the foundation of the practice and that you have a goal of making the SOPs better. In meetings, reinforce the idea that you value their opinions and are happy to hear their suggestions for updates.

I've found that it can be effective to incentivize team members with a bonus when they suggest a helpful update to an SOP so that they stay alert to ways you might improve your processes.

Sometimes, your team will make suggestions that are valid, but not a major priority—it's your job as the owner to take all that input and filter it based on a larger strategy. But it's key to not make your team member feel as though they got something "wrong" by suggesting a small change that isn't a priority. This could discourage your entire team from coming forward with suggestions out of a fear of failure.

Beyond SOPs, the following need to be updated regularly:

- Questionnaires
- Document templates
- Custom fields and custom field sets in your practice management software
- Automations

As you run your practice, you're always getting feedback from both your clients and your team. Your clients may have trouble with a certain step of the process, and multiple clients coming to you with the same question is a red flag that there's an area where you can make a change. Your team will notice pain points in the technology as they carry out their tasks. They might make observations such as, "I got a response, but it didn't come in a PDF" or "On our questionnaire, we only have one box to write the name of the client's orthopedic surgeon, but this client has two. If we add a capability to write multiple doctors, our clients might give us more complete information." This sort of feedback in invaluable in consistently improving systems.

Your goal is to operate a zero-friction practice, and as time goes on, your clients and team will alert you to the friction points that are getting in their way. As you discover more of these friction points (and move from tackling larger friction points to tackling smaller friction points), you'll be able to run your business more smoothly.

You'll also need to update your processes to reflect changes in the law or in the Social Security Administration's requirements. For example, when the Social Security Administration implemented the National Uniformity Rule "5-day letter", we needed to update our task list and document template to accommodate this change. While it's certainly easier to keep the status quo, we know that change is constant. Remember when they withheld the hearing ALJ's identity prior the hearing? That was an interesting time. Thankfully, that changed.

On Perfectionism

When it comes to running a law firm, perfectionism is not the answer.

Making changes and updates is a normal part of running a business. Like a car needs maintenance, your practice's operations need maintenance. Discovering friction points or changing an SOP isn't a "failure." It's a necessary and frequent step to refining your practice. The goal is continued progress, not perfection.

Your practice is your masterpiece. No masterpiece was completed in a day... It'll take years of subtle improvements to gradually get it where you want it to be. If you try to get everything perfect on the first try, you're setting yourself up for failure.

Maintaining Momentum

When you begin the process of transforming your practice, the excitement of starting will propel you. But after a few months, the adrenaline will wane, and you'll realize how much hard work lies ahead. I've seen many attorneys reach this point and slowly stagnate, not following through on implementing changes.

To sustain momentum, it's helpful to have a guide to hold you accountable and prompt you to take action. A guide makes this process easy... If you get lost and overwhelmed, your guide is there to keep you on track and say, "Okay, here's the next step. Let's do this." Like most good things in life, the joy comes after the hard part. But the trick is sticking it out through the hard part and coming out the other side... A guide reduces the odds that you'll give up on making these changes when you get exhausted.

There are a number of guides that can help give you direction and hold you accountable. Throughout my career, I have worked with many mentors, colleagues, online communities, masterminds, consultants and coaches.

CHAPTER 12

Life on the Other Side...

When you run a proactive, calm disability law firm, this is what life can look like:

Yes, that's me, hiking—on a Wednesday afternoon.

At the very moment this picture was taken, my law firm was operating smoothly without me, just like a normal

Wednesday. My team was using their Standard Operating Procedures (SOPs) to complete their tasks without needing my input, and my clients were being served.

Years ago, if you'd told me that I would be able to take an afternoon away from my law firm to go hiking, paddleboarding, or any of the other things I love to do outside of work, I would have looked at you like you were crazy. "Who is going to do all this work? What if a client needs to talk to me? I have so much on my mind that it's hard to sleep most nights..."

But when you implement systems and processes that your team can operate without you, you free up your schedule to finally enjoy your life.

Maybe hiking isn't your thing. But with the hours you free up, you could go to the spa, play golf, volunteer at your daughter's school, you name it...

If you want to take time off to visit family or take a beach vacation, you no longer have to wait for a miracle to happen. With your team handling most of the day-to-day operations of your firm (and with SOPs that make it easy for a team member to pick up your tasks while you're away), the only thing tethering you to your law firm is your cases—and with virtual hearings becoming the new normal, you have the ultimate flexibility. If you wanted to, you could work from anywhere. You have options that you didn't have before.

Now, there are three doors you could walk through—and all of them lead to fantastic lives. Let's stop for a moment and appreciate that: most lawyers never get to the point where they evaluate these choices. Most remain stuck on the "hamster wheel," just trying to survive another work week.

The Three Doors

If you implement the things that we've discussed in the book there are three doors that you could walk through and *all of them* lead to fantastic lives.

Door 1: If you're happy working the number of hours you're working now, you can continue doing that. But now, you'll make a lot more money because you'll be more efficient and can handle more clients in the same number of hours (with less stress).

Door 2: If you want to prioritize having more time away from the office, you can focus on taking fewer clients, while increasing your effective hourly rate because you're so much more efficient.

Door 3: Maybe you no longer want to practice law at all… Now that your system and processes are documented, you can hire attorneys to take your place, while you become the CEO of your business. This tends to be a win-win situation for both you and the attorneys you hire. Many attorneys have no interest in running a business but want the autonomy of running their own firms. With you as CEO, these attorneys don't have to worry about big-picture business decisions, while you can step away from your role as an attorney—and still profit from the business you built.

None of these doors are better than the others, so your decision comes down to what you want. How do you envision the rest of your life? How do you want to spend your time? The choice is yours.

No matter which choice you make—the suffering is over!

Say goodbye to the endless, stressful days of the phone ringing off the hook while you struggle to make progress on an insurmountable mountain of work. Finally, you can wake up in the morning and feel excitement, not dread about your day. You actually have time to take care of your physical, mental, and emotional needs, and you can finally enjoy quality time with the ones you love.

You started your own law firm because you wanted to do things your way. You wanted to run the show and have more autonomy, more freedom, more time, and more money. The law firm grind quickly got in your way—but now, you can finally have all of those things you envisioned when you launched your firm.

No matter which direction you decide to take your career and your life, the future belongs to you.

CONCLUSION

You've seen a glimpse of what the future could look like... But if you don't take action, it'll remain nothing but a fantasy.

Making these changes is a months or years-long process. It will require hard work and determination, but the payoff will make it all worth it. Along the way, you'll need to stay focused on your end goal of having a business you love to run and a lifestyle that makes you happy.

It can be intimidating to start this journey, but you have to start somewhere. I encourage you to take the first small step to changing your law firm. Each successive step will get easier and easier, and you'll build momentum that eventually carries you to the finish line.

A brief warning: some readers may close this book, go to work tomorrow morning, and carry on exactly as they did before. They'll slide right back into the breakneck pace and never-ending slog of running a law firm—but they'll be tortured by the thought that everything could be different. That in another life, they could be working less, making more money, and enjoying the freedom of running a law firm wherever and whenever they want.

Knowing what you know now, could you ever go back to the old way of running your law firm? Could you endure the endless hours, tense environment, and draining grind now that you know life could be better?

I know that I couldn't. The moment I realized I had to change my life as a law firm owner, I couldn't rest until I made it happen. It felt like someone had thrown me a lifeline. Just a few years later, I'd gone from rock bottom to the happiest, healthiest, and most profitable I'd been in my life.

I hope this book can be the same lifeline for you.

ABOUT THE AUTHOR

Maria Bermudez is the founder of Disability Advocacy Group, LLC, a legal consulting and advocacy practice based out of San Juan, Puerto Rico. Maria spent the first 15 years of her practice in Philadelphia focusing exclusively on Social Security and Long-Term Disability benefits under ERISA plans. She also worked in Philadelphia as an Attorney Advisor for Region 3 under the direction of the Regional Chief Judge. Maria has handled thousands of cases from inception through federal court and provides consulting services to fellow colleagues in the areas of law firm operations and infrastructure.

Maria previously served as the co-chair of the Philadelphia Bar Association's Social Security Disability Committee in addition to a number of non-profit and professional organization leadership positions over the years. Maria is licensed in the Third Circuit, and all federal courts in Pennsylvania, New Jersey, and Puerto Rico.

Maria's published includes co-authoring the American Bar Associations Administrative Proceedings Bench Book in 2012 with respect to HIV in Social Security proceedings. Maria was published by ABA in the Law Practice Today, authoring: Paper or Plastic? A column focusing on technology use in administrative proceedings. She was published by The Legal Intelligencer, authoring a peach on The Significance of Writing in the Legal Setting. Finally, Maria wrote Monthly Columns in the Philadelphia Bar Reporter during her tenure as a young lawyer focusing establishing a network, leadership and embracing change.

Maria's passion for infrastructure and technology is rooted in a heartfelt desire to improve the quality of life of practitioners in this area while balancing the quality of service the disabled community deserves.

To explore Maria's preferred tools and essential resources, visit www.disabilityadvocacygroup.com.

www.ingramcontent.com/pod-product-compliance
Lightning Source LLC
Chambersburg PA
CBHW071608200326
41519CB00021BB/6915